The First Ladies Hall

THE NATIONAL MUSEUM OF HISTORY AND TECHNOLOGY

SMITHSONIAN INSTITUTION

SMITHSONIAN INSTITUTION PRESS · WASHINGTON, D.C.

The text of this booklet was prepared in consultation with Margaret Brown Klapthor, curator of political history, The National Museum of History and Technology, Smithsonian Institution.

LIBRARY OF CONGRESS CATALOGING IN PUBLICATION DATA

National Museum of History and Technology.
The First Ladies Hall.

1. *Costume—United States—History.*
2. *Presidents—United States—Wives. I. Title.*
GT605.N27   391'.07'20973   73-8675
ISBN 0-87474-133-5

10   9   8   7

Introduction

Dresses worn by First Ladies of every administration from that of President Washington to the present are exhibited in the First Ladies Hall in the National Museum of History and Technology.

The idea for this collection originated in the early 1900s with Mrs. Rose Gouverneur Hoes and Mrs. Julian James, two Washington women who were interested in the costumes collections of the Smithsonian Institution. Mrs. William Howard Taft presented the first dress to the Smithsonian in 1912 when she was the First Lady. Former First Ladies and their descendants all over the United States then began to donate dresses, and every subsequent First Lady has followed suit.

The dresses are displayed on mannequins whose faces are identical, modeled after a bust representing Cordelia, daughter of Shakespeare's King Lear, made in 1863 by sculptor Pierce F. Connelly of Louisiana. The bust, which is pictured above, can be seen in the First Ladies Hall. The expression of the eyes of each mannequin, the hair styles, the coloring, and the sizes of the figures themselves are different—all based as closely as possible on photographs, paintings, statues, or written descriptions of the individual First Ladies.

The First Lady has not always been the President's wife. For various reasons, a relative or friend has sometimes performed the duties of official White House hostess.

The collection is installed in period room settings that display the dresses in the types of surroundings in which they were originally worn. In creating these settings the Museum has used, wherever possible, actual architectural details and fixtures of the White House itself, and furniture and furnishings owned by Presidents of the United States.

Since each room setting contains dresses representing a span of several administrations, it has been necessary to select a style of background and furnishings typical of a certain period or of a single administration within a period. Changes in White House decoration are shown in these settings, which are based wherever possible on written descriptions and pictorial evidence of the White House. Thus, the hall reflects changing styles of interior decoration as well as changes in fashion since 1789.

Also on display in the First Ladies Hall is the most complete collection of White House china outside of the Executive Mansion. It includes pieces of table service used in every administration.

Changes are made in the room settings from time to time to improve the First Ladies exhibit, and sometimes dresses must be removed for renovation.

Martha Washington *Abigail Adams* *Martha Randolph*

As you enter the First Ladies Hall the first room setting represents the second-floor parlor of the Executive Mansion in Philadelphia, which was the national capital from 1790 to 1800.

The room is arranged with furniture and accessories —silver Argand lamps, porcelain, silver, glass, mirror, oil painting—that were used by President and Mrs. Washington at Mount Vernon and in their Presidential residences. The mantelpiece is a replica of the drawing room mantel in the Philadelphia mansion, and the rug with the Great Seal of the United States was actually used there.

MARTHA CUSTIS WASHINGTON, the *first* First Lady, is seated beside her tea table, wearing a dress of salmon-pink faille, handpainted with a design of native North American wildflowers in the larger medallion spaces and insects in the smaller ones. Mrs. Washington herself made the brown satin bag she is holding. It is embroidered in ribbonwork with the inscription "Worn by Genl G & Mrs Washington" worked across the front. The mob cap she wears was fashionable for social gatherings in the late eighteenth century.

ABIGAIL SMITH ADAMS's dress of brocaded silk was worn when she was in England where John Adams served as the first American minister, 1785–1788. She then sent it to her sister, Mary Smith Cranch of Haverhill, Massachusetts, who helped care for the two younger Adams sons during their parents' absence in Europe.

The eighteenth-century quilted petticoat is a replacement; an eighteenth-century gauze kerchief fashionably arranged completes the outfit. The brooch contains locks of Abigail Adams's hair, along with those of her husband, John, and of her son, President John Quincy Adams.

MARTHA JEFFERSON RANDOLPH often served as hostess for her father, who had been a widower for eighteen years when he took office as President. Although no

dress worn by Mrs. Randolph could be found, she is represented in this setting in a long Paisley shawl that belonged to her. It measures about 8 by 4 feet and is made of fine black wool, with the border woven in oriental design.

Brown satin bag made by Martha Washington. The Lewis Collection.

Martha Washington's green velvet mitt.

1789–1809

Administrations of George Washington
John Adams · Thomas Jefferson

Parlor, Executive Mansion, Philadelphia

From left to right: Mrs. Washington, Mrs. Adams, and Mrs. Randolph.

To the right of the entrance doorway into the First Ladies Hall is a bedroom (opposite page) as it may have looked in the Philadelphia Executive Mansion. It is furnished with some of the great variety of President and Mrs. Washington's household furnishings to be found in the Smithsonian collections.

The wing chair was in George Washington's bedroom at Mount Vernon. The Chippendale bed, the oriental export porcelain water bottle and bowl and the dressing mirror are also from Mount Vernon. President Washington carried the brass candlestick with him on his travels for use in reading and correspondence. It provided illumination while he drafted his Farewell Address to the nation.

These oil portraits of George and Martha Washington are miniatures painted from life by the American artist, John Trumbull, about 1795.

The Washington Bedroom

Dolley Madison   *Elizabeth Monroe*   *Maria Gouverneur*   *Louisa Adams*

The tall figure at right in this setting of a White House music room as it might have looked about 1825 is DOLLEY PAYNE MADISON, who has gone down in history as one of the most popular of First Ladies, and is renowned for having saved a number of valuables from the White House when the mansion was burned by the British during the War of 1812.

Mrs. Madison's gown is Empire style with a high waistline. A contemporary account by Mrs. Benjamin Crowninshield, wife of the Secretary of the Navy, described the dress as "yellow satin embroidered all over with sprigs of butterflies, not two alike. . . ." It was worn by Mrs. Madison to the New Year's Day reception in 1816.

Turbans were fashionable at the beginning of the nineteenth century, and Dolley Madison, who had worn a Quaker cap in her youth, always wore a turban at public functions. The sandlewood fan belonged to her.

The dress, second from the right in this setting, was probably one worn by Mrs. Lawrence Kortright, the mother of ELIZABETH KORTRIGHT MONROE, a dress treasured as a family heirloom. It is of the "saque" period and is made of deep-cream taffeta brocaded with large bunches of flowers; the back features a Watteau pleat. The handsome topaz necklace, composed of eighteen oval-shaped stones, was a gift to his wife from President James Monroe, while he was Minister to France.

Standing next to her is the Monroes' daughter, MARIA MONROE GOUVERNEUR, who was still living with her family when her father became President. Her marriage at the age of 17 in 1820 to her cousin, Samuel L. Gouverneur, one of President Monroe's secretaries, was the first wedding of a President's daughter in the White House.

Mrs. Gouverneur's gown is of pale blue silk in the late Empire style. It is trimmed with straw embroidery, which was made by splitting the straw of ordinary wheat and applying it to the material with an embroidery technique. The effect resembles the finest of glossy silk thread.

LOUISA JOHNSON ADAMS, at left, was born in England of an American father and an English mother. She is the only First Lady to have been born abroad. She had also lived abroad for many years while her husband, President John Quincy Adams, oldest son of the second President, was in the diplomatic service.

Mrs. Adams's dress has a bell-shaped skirt and a high waistline in the Empire style. It is made of white net festooned with silver braid worn over a white satin underdress. The linen handkerchief shown with this dress measures a yard square, but fine material and dainty embroidery give it a feminine appearance.

The harp, music stand, and books belonged to Mrs. Adams, and the piano was in the White House during the Adams administration. The gold armchair is from the French suite of furniture purchased by President Monroe for the Oval Drawing Room of the White House.

1809–1829

Administrations of James Madison
James Monroe · John Quincy Adams

Music Room

From left to right: Mrs. Adams, Mrs. Gouverneur, Mrs. Monroe, and Mrs. Madison.

Emily Donelson

Sarah Jackson

Angelica Van Buren

Jane Findlay

Julia Tyler

In this setting, which resembles a White House reception room as it might have looked during the Van Buren administration (1838–1841), both the dresses and the furnishings show a transition from Empire to Victorian taste in decoration.

The wallpaper was inspired by a contemporary description of a White House room that told of "white paper sprinkled with gold stars and a gilt border." The silk oriental rug was a gift to President Martin Van Buren from the Imam of Muscat. The eagle-back side chair was also in the Executive Mansion in this period. Other furniture and accessories are of a type that was popular in this country in the early nineteenth century.

The earliest inaugural gown in the collection is worn by the figure at right, representing EMILY TENNESSEE DONELSON, who served as First Lady for her widower uncle, President Andrew Jackson. Legend has it that the dress—made of gold satin brocaded with a design of rosebuds and violets—was a gift from him. The short puffed sleeves and tight-fitting bodice were very fashionable at that time.

The skirt of the original gown was destroyed by fire in an accident before the dress came to the Museum and the present skirt is a restoration, decorated with blond lace that had belonged to Mrs. Andrew Jackson. Mrs. Donelson's elaborate hairdo was dictated by the fashion of the period.

In 1836 Mrs. Donelson became too ill to continue her duties as First Lady so SARAH YORKE JACKSON, young bride of the President's adopted son, assumed the role. One of the most diminutive of the First Ladies, she is represented (second from right) in her wedding dress, which she wore when presented to Washington society at a reception and dinner shortly after her arrival at the White House. The dress has a white mull skirt, embroidered with silk floss in a floral design, and a bodice of white satin.

There was no official hostess for Martin Van Buren, a widower, when he became President. The following year, however, his oldest son married fashionable Angelica Singleton, who then took over as First Lady. The dress of ANGELICA VAN BUREN (center) is the first to illustrate the hoop skirt—that all-prevailing mode of the mid-nineteenth century. The royal blue gown with its long train is dramatic in effect. The heavy skirt, which measures 8 to 10 yards around the hem, is supported by a foundation skirt and a set of hoops that were originally worn with the dress. An ostrich plume in Mrs. Van Buren's dark hair and a forehead jewel complete the regal picture.

Because President William Henry Harrison's ailing wife was unable to travel from Ohio at the time he was elected, he asked his widowed daughter-in-law, Jane Irwin Harrison, to act as First Lady. She was assisted by her foster mother, JANE IRWIN FINDLAY, who was then 73.

Because no dress belonging to the young Mrs. Harrison could be found for the collection, the gown worn by Mrs. Findlay at the Harrison inaugural ball represents that administration. It is a rather quaint dress of dark-brown velvet with leg-of-mutton sleeves.

Next is a dress worn by the second wife of President John Tyler, JULIA GARDINER TYLER (far left). The first Mrs. Tyler, an invalid, died in the White House, and in 1844 the President married Julia Gardiner, a society belle from New York City, who was some 30 years younger. This was the first marriage of a President while in office.

Mrs. Tyler's gown is the one she wore in 1841 when presented at the French court. It is made of sheer white mull, and the bodice and three flounces of the skirt are embroidered with silver thread and a pastel flower design.

1829–1845

Administrations of
Andrew Jackson · Martin Van Buren
William Henry Harrison · John Tyler

Reception Room

From left to right: Mrs. Tyler, Mrs. Findlay, Mrs. Van Buren, Mrs. Jackson, and Mrs. Donelson.

1845–1869

Administrations of James K. Polk
Zachary Taylor · Millard Fillmore
Franklin Pierce · James Buchanan
Abraham Lincoln · Andrew Johnson

Sarah Polk

Betty Bliss

Abigail Fillmore

Jane Pierce

Harriet Lane

Mary Lincoln

Martha Patterson

Victorian Parlor

From left to right: Mrs. Patterson, Mrs. Pierce, Mrs. Lincoln, Mrs. Fillmore, Mrs. Bliss, Harriet Lane, and Mrs. Polk. (Victorian Parlor text, including descriptions of these First Ladies' dresses, is on the following page.)

The photograph on the preceding pages represents a parlor as it might have looked in the White House during the mid-nineteenth century.

The wallpaper was reproduced from a small piece of original White House paper found under several layers of plaster and paneling while the Executive Mansion was being renovated during the Truman administration. Original White House pieces include the marble mantel, installed during the Pierce administration, and the silver service on the table, which belonged to Mrs. Abraham Lincoln.

The elaborately carved furniture of laminated rosewood was probably made by Alexander Roux, a fine New York cabinetmaker of the mid-nineteenth-century period. Furniture similar to this was used in the White House in the mid-nineteenth century. The cloverleaf sofa is also typical of that period.

It was the era of the hoop skirt—as the dresses illustrate. SARAH CHILDRESS POLK (far right), who actively advised and assisted her husband, President James A. Polk, in his career, is wearing her inaugural ball gown of 1845. It is made of blue ribbed silk damask with a poinsettia design.

Mrs. Zachary Taylor, preferring the seclusion of her room, left the duties of First Lady to her daughter, BETTY TAYLOR BLISS, the recent bride of her father's adjutant, Major William W. Bliss. "Miss Betty," as she was known, is standing at right of the window, wearing a daytime dress of greenish-brown grenadine trimmed with plaid borders. This is the last dress in the collection to have been made entirely by hand, for in 1846 the sewing machine was invented and all the later dresses have some machine sewing on them.

Standing at left of the window is ABIGAIL POWERS FILLMORE who, as a young woman, became both teacher and inspiration to Millard Fillmore, the man she was to marry and see win the Presidency. Educated and cultured, Mrs. Fillmore was instrumental in establishing the first library in the White House. She is wearing a lavender taffeta dress with a brocade flounce. The handkerchief ring is an interesting costume accessory of the period.

The black dress worn by JANE APPLETON PIERCE is a keynote to the social life of the White House during the administration of President Franklin Pierce. Mrs. Pierce was in mourning for their only son, who was killed in an accident at the age of 12 shortly after the Presidential election. Her dress is made of black tulle embroidered with silver dots, worn over a black taffeta underdress. A little jacket of tulle and silver at first glance appears to be part of the dress itself. Mrs. Pierce holds the ends of the jacket. Her black lace and net cap is trimmed with velvet, jet beads, and gold.

First Lady during the administration of President James Buchanan, the only bachelor President, was his attractive niece, HARRIET LANE (JOHNSTON). In contrast to the restricted social life of the previous Pierce administration, this one was gay and charming. Miss Lane, though young, was entirely equal to the demands of the position of First Lady, even presiding without flaw during the visit of the Prince of Wales (later Edward VII of England) as a houseguest at the White House.

Miss Lane is represented (second from right) in her wedding dress of white moire taffeta trimmed with white satin and lace. The bridal veil of point lace is draped over the head of the mannequin. Miss Lane married Henry Elliot Johnston in 1866, a few years after her uncle had retired from public life.

The dress worn by MARY TODD LINCOLN, the central figure in the room, is made of royal purple velvet. The seams are piped with white satin and each panel of the full skirt is of a different width. Mrs. Lincoln had a special fondness for clothes and chose her accessories with taste and care. Accompanying the dress are a fan made of purple silk and a matching parasol. The dainty gold wrist watch, which belonged to Mrs. Lincoln, is a very early and elegant example of this utilitarian accessory.

The horrors of the Civil War, domestic bereavement, and the fact that she was not accepted socially in Washington, then largely a city of Southerners, made Mrs. Lincoln's White House years unhappy. She vented her frustrations in an orgy of spending—buying handsome clothes and beautiful accessories for herself and elegant furnishings for the White House.

At far left in this room setting is MARTHA JOHNSON PATTERSON, daughter of President Andrew Johnson and wife of United States Senator David T. Patterson. She acted as First Lady in place of her invalid mother—and her calm, diplomatic tact made her a valuable asset to her father during his rather stormy administration.

Mrs. Patterson is not represented here by a dress, but instead by an evening cloak, known as a "burnous," which she wore during her White House years. It is made of finely woven wool, ornamented with gold braid and tassels, and has a gold tasseled hood, which may be worn over the head or pushed back.

The photograph on the following pages shows the Blue Room of the White House as it looked during the administration of President Ulysses S. Grant, and is based on contemporary photographs. Both the lavish decorations of the room and the heavily embroidered and beaded dresses characterize the period.

The gold furniture was purchased during President James Buchanan's administration, and was used in the Blue Room until 1902. A portrait of President Grant by William Cogswell hangs over the black marble mantel, which was installed in the White House—but not in the Blue Room—during the Grant administration. The large porcelain vase, decorated with orchids and butterflies, beside the mantel belonged to Mrs. Benjamin Harrison. Cloisonné vases on the mantel were given to the Grants on their round-the-world tour.

At far right is the dress JULIA DENT GRANT wore to President Grant's second inaugural ball of 1873. It is made of white-and-silver brocade, a gift from the Emperor of China. This gown illustrates the transition period when fashion was gradually changing from the hoop skirt to the bustle. The lace fichu around the shoulder was worn at the inaugural ball of 1869 by Mrs. Grant, who described her years as First Lady as the happiest of her life.

LUCY WEBB HAYES (second from right), the first college graduate to preside as First Lady, wears the first dress in the collection made in the elaborate style of the late nineteenth-century bustle period, with a train and elaborate trimmings of lace, fringe, and beads. Because Mrs. Hayes disliked the low necklines then fashionable, soft net fills the neck opening.

There was no Hayes inaugural ball because the contested close election did not allow enough time for one to be organized. Instead, Mrs. Hayes wore this gown at a state dinner given at the White House for the Grand Duke Alexis of Russia during the administration of President Rutherford B. Hayes.

LUCRETIA RUDOLPH GARFIELD is represented by the gown (third from right) that she wore at President James A. Garfield's 1881 inaugural ball, which was held in the Smithsonian's Arts and Industries Building. The original lavender has faded to soft gray. Instead of trimmings and beads and fringe, this dress of the bustle period is trimmed with lace, ribbons, and ruchings made of the same fabric as the dress.

Because President Chester A. Arthur's wife had died before he came to office, his sister, MARY ARTHUR MCELROY, presided as hostess during his administration. Her dress (fourth from right) is of gray satin damask with a morning glory design. The skirt is gored with fullness at the back, but there is no bustle.

Grover Cleveland was a bachelor when he became President, and for a little more than a year of his first administration his sister, ROSE ELIZABETH CLEVELAND, a teacher, author, lecturer, and advocate of women's rights, acted as First Lady. Her dress (third from left) is made of garnet red silk velvet. Light pink faille creates a contrast at the neckline and the skirt inserts. Trimming consists of heavy silver-and-gold braid.

CAROLINE SCOTT HARRISON (second from left) decided that on such an American occasion as an inaugural ball she should wear a dress entirely of American manufacture. Material for the dress was especially woven by the Logan Silk Company, and the design of gray satin was taken from Indiana's burr oaks, which are especially numerous on the battleground at Tippecanoe, the scene of glory of President Benjamin Harrison's grandfather, William Henry Harrison.

The bodice and skirt are made of silver-gray faille, and the front panels of the skirt are made of gray satin. Each panel is edged with apricot silk veiled with lace. The collar and trimmings are of silver and gold-bead fringe. This dress is an excellent example of the elaborate materials and trimmings worn during the bustle period.

Mrs. Harrison died in 1892 during her husband's administration. MARY HARRISON MCKEE, the Harrisons' daughter, then assumed the duties of hostess. Her dress (far left) is the one she had worn at her father's inaugural ball in 1889—and it is also entirely of American design and manufacture, including the material.

It, too, is an elaborate gown of the bustle period, made of parchment-colored satin, brocaded with a goldenrod design in gold and olive. She selected the design as a compliment to her father whose favorite flower was goldenrod. The front of the skirt is made of gold taffeta opening over an underskirt of apple-green velvet. A network of amber and silver beads decorates the bodice front.

1869–1893

Administrations of Ulysses S. Grant
Rutherford B. Hayes · James A. Garfield
Chester A. Arthur · Grover Cleveland
Benjamin Harrison

Blue Room I

Julia Grant

Lucy Hayes

Lucretia Garfield

Mary McElroy

Rose Cleveland

Caroline Harrison

Mary McKee

From left to right: Mrs. McKee, Mrs. Harrison, Rose Elizabeth Cleveland, Mrs. McElroy, Mrs. Garfield, Mrs. Hayes, and Mrs. Grant. (Blue Room I text, including descriptions of these First Ladies' dresses, is on the preceding page.)

Frances Cleveland

Ida McKinley

Edith Roosevelt

Helen Taft

Ellen Wilson

Edith Wilson

By the end of the nineteenth century, the Blue Room had been redecorated in robin's-egg blue, and the style of the decoration had changed to the sophisticated elegance of this setting. The gold furniture purchased in 1859 was still in use, but had been reupholstered to match the new color scheme. The two eagle-design glass globes on the front branches of the gas chandelier were used in the White House during this period.

The figure representing Frances Folsom Cleveland (left) has one hand outstretched in typical cordial greeting. She had been married to President Grover Cleveland at the age of 22 in the Blue Room in 1886 during his first term in office, thus becoming the only First Lady ever to have been married in the White House.

Her dress is one that she wore during her husband's second administration. The iridescent taffeta of the underskirt and bodice is brocaded with a black overlay design giving the appearance of lace. The black satin overskirt and bodice are trimmed with jet beads and black sequins, and a fur band borders the skirt.

The beautiful fabrics and elaborate styling of the inaugural-ball gowns of the next three First Ladies—Mrs. William McKinley, Mrs. Theodore Roosevelt, and Mrs. William Howard Taft—are especially handsome.

The gown worn by Ida Saxton McKinley (second from left) at President McKinley's second inaugural ball is of heavy white satin, and the front panel of the skirt is embroidered with pearls. Rose-point lace trims bodice, skirt, and sleeves. The high, tight collar was a distinctive fashion note of the time.

The gown worn by Edith Kermit Carow Roosevelt (third from left) at President Theodore Roosevelt's inaugural ball of 1905 is made of robin's-egg blue brocade with a design of swallows and pinwheels of gold. The material was especially designed for her and woven in Paterson, New Jersey.

During this period, skirts began to fall in an easy graceful sweep over the hips, forming broad undulations about the feet. The simple square-cut neckline is edged with heirloom rose-point lace. Mrs. Roosevelt wore a rose diamond necklace like the one displayed with the dress, and a blue aigrette feather in her hair.

Helen Herron Taft (third from right) is represented in the gown she wore at President Taft's inaugural ball of 1909. It was designed during a revival of the Empire fashion, with high waistline, clinging skirt, and a train.

Made of white silk chiffon, which Mrs. Taft had sent to Tokyo to be embroidered, the dress was the first to be received for the Smithsonian collection. It was the generosity and interest of Mrs. Taft, then presiding as First Lady, that got the collection of First Ladies' dresses off to such a fine start.

The dress of Ellen Axson Wilson (second from right) is made of white brocaded velvet in a rose design. The skirt is draped about the hips, and the narrow hobble skirt (an outstanding fashion feature of the day) is split up the knee over the white satin-and-lace underskirt with its short, sharp train. The bodice has a net yoke embroidered with rhinestones, steel beads, seed pearls, and large baroque pearls.

After his first wife's death in 1914, only a year after his administration had begun, President Woodrow Wilson married Edith Bolling Galt the following fall. When he became seriously ill in 1919, the second Mrs. Wilson was his constant companion and assistant. Her black velvet dress (far right) was part of her trousseau and later was worn by her during the Paris Peace Conference of 1919. It has a narrow skirt, and the long train is part of the tunic overdress. Jet sequins and jet-bead tassels provide ornamentation. The black is unrelieved except for a single line of green beads bordering the jet sequins at the neckline.

The dresses worn by the first Mrs. Wilson and the second Mrs. Wilson are representative of the transition period between the stylized fashions of the nineteenth century and the more fluid lines of the twentieth century.

1893–1921

Administrations of Grover Cleveland
William McKinley · Theodore Roosevelt
William Howard Taft · Woodrow Wilson

Blue Room II

From left to right: Mrs. Cleveland, Mrs. McKinley, Mrs. Roosevelt, Mrs. Taft, Mrs. Ellen Axson Wilson, and Mrs. Edith Bolling Wilson.

Florence Harding   *Grace Coolidge*   *Lou Hoover*

1921–1961

Administrations of Warren G. Harding
Calvin Coolidge · Herbert Hoover
Franklin D. Roosevelt · Harry S Truman
Dwight D. Eisenhower

East Room

From left to right: Mrs. Harding, Mrs. Coolidge, Mrs. Hoover, Mrs. Roosevelt, Mrs. Truman, Mrs. Eisenhower. (East Room text, including descriptions of these First Ladies' dresses, is on the following page.)

Eleanor Roosevelt

Bess Truman

Mamie Eisenhower

The photograph on the preceding pages represents the East Room of the White House combining architectural features installed during the renovation in 1902 by the firm of McKim, Mead and White, with interior decoration added during the renovation of the White House in 1952 during the Truman administration. The wood panelling and pilasters, the marble mantels, and one of the gold mirror frames were actually in the East Room of the White House from 1902 to 1952. The gold curtains are made in the style and of the fabric chosen for the Truman renovation.

The gold furniture which dates back to the administration of James Buchanan was removed from the Blue Room in 1902, but continued to be used in the White House from then until it came to the Smithsonian Institution in 1937. This furniture can be seen in a photograph taken of the East Room during the administration of President Herbert Hoover. The famous gold concert grand piano (Steinway #100,000) was a present to the United States Government in 1903 for use in the East Room of the White House. The case is decorated with the seals of the thirteen original colonies and the painting under the lid is by the American impressionist artist, Thomas Dewing.

At far left is the satin dress worn by FLORENCE KLING HARDING to a social event shortly after President Warren Harding's inauguration in 1921. The bodice is heavily embroidered with rhinestones and baroque pearls. The drape of the skirt shows the upward trend that dresses were taking at that time. This is the first figure to have the feet exposed, revealing white satin slippers with pointed toes, French heels, and rhinestone buckles.

Mrs. Harding opened the White House for entertaining again after it had been closed to social functions during the years of World War I and President Wilson's subsequent illness.

Typical of the "flapper" period of the 1920s is the red chiffon velvet dress of GRACE GOODHUE COOLIDGE (second from left). It features a plain sleeveless bodice, U-neckline, hip-length waistline, and a skirt made of three tiers. A long train is attached at the shoulders. Matching slippers have rhinestone buckles and gold heels.

The warmth and friendliness of Mrs. Coolidge's personality were an ideal foil for "silent Cal," as President Calvin Coolidge was popularly known. Her charm, tact, and gaiety made her one of the most popular of White House hostesses.

The dress of LOU HENRY HOOVER (third from left) is made of lustrous pale-green satin that falls into bias folds and drapes. Typical of the early 1930s, it has a draped cowl neckline, cap sleeves, and a cord-belted low waistline. Two rhinestone clips, one on each shoulder, are the only ornamentation.

ANNA ELEANOR ROOSEVELT is represented in a gown (fourth from left) that she wore at the celebration of Franklin D. Roosevelt's inauguration on the evening of January 20, 1941. At the President's request there was no ball. Instead, a concert in honor of the occasion was given in Constitution Hall. The gown is made of satin that varies in color from ivory to deep peach, depending on the light. The neckline and sleeves are trimmed with tinted pearls of the same color. A double train from the shoulders widens to several yards at the hem and falls into the full skirt. Mrs. Roosevelt traveled tirelessly, acting as eyes and ears for her handicapped husband, during his administration as President. Her humanitarian activities both in the White House and in her later years endeared her to people all over the world.

BESS WALLACE TRUMAN (fifth from left) wore this dress of smoke gray mousseline de soie at a state dinner that she and President Harry S Truman gave for Queen Juliana of the Netherlands on April 2, 1952. The dinner was held at the Sheraton-Carlton Hotel because the White House was undergoing major renovations at the time.

Mrs. Truman concentrated her time as First Lady on the more traditional roles of wife of the President and mother of the Trumans' only child, Margaret. Mrs. Truman's opinions, shared privately with the President, were very important to him and her influence was greater than was generally recognized by the American public.

MAMIE DOUD EISENHOWER (sixth from left) was dressed in pink, her favorite color, at President Dwight D. Eisenhower's first inaugural ball. Designed by Nettie Rosenstein of New York, the gown is of pink peau de soie with a mauve undertone, and is embroidered with more than 2,000 rhinestones. Accessories are of matching pink fabric, including the evening bag, also designed by Nettie Rosenstein. The fabric of this silver-framed bag is encrusted with 3,456 pink rhinestones, pearls, and beads.

Mrs. Eisenhower's friendly manner and ready smile endeared her to the American people. She enjoyed living in the White House, being the wife of the President, and serving as First Lady of the land.

Administration of John F. Kennedy
Lyndon B. Johnson · Richard M. Nixon
Gerald Ford · Jimmy Carter · Ronald Reagan

Red Room

The photograph on the following page represents the Red Room of the White House as it looked after its renovation by Mrs. John F. Kennedy and the Fine Arts Committee she appointed to assist her in the redecoration of the White House. Furnished as an Empire Parlor of the period 1810–1830, the Red Room was presented to the public in 1962 as the first of the State Rooms to be done by Mrs. Kennedy and the Committee. In recreating the room setting at the Smithsonian, the walls have been hung with the same handsome cerise silk with gold borders used in the White House room. From the White House were lent the curtains used in the room and the Savonnerie carpet of the Empire period. The White House also made available the French desk with ormolu mounts which stands next to the window, as well as the convex mirror with the eagle pediment which hangs over the desk and the card table supported by a gilt winged sphinx. The table is flanked with American Empire side chairs of the 1820s. All of these pieces were in the Red Room in the White House. From the Smithsonian's collections has been added the Empire sofa and the art works in the room. The large painting in the center of the back wall showing Mrs. Herbert Hoover and her dogs on the south lawn of the White House was executed by Franklin Clark in 1932.

The white silk dress worn by JACQUELINE BOUVIER KENNEDY (far right) at President John F. Kennedy's inaugural ball in 1961 was made by designer Ethel Frankau of the Custom Salon, Bergdorf Goodman, based on ideas and sketches from Mrs. Kennedy.

It has a bodice embroidered in silver thread, and is veiled overall with a layer of white chiffon to give a soft, shimmering effect. A floor-length cape of the same silk is triple-layered with chiffon. It buttons at the neck with an embroidered frog on a military collar.

The classically simple inaugural ball gown worn by CLAUDIA (LADY BIRD) TAYLOR JOHNSON (second from right) at President Lyndon B. Johnson's inaugural ball in 1965 is made of jonquil-yellow double-woven satin, and was designed by American couturier John Moore.

The coat is of matching fabric with a standing collar and three-quarter-length sleeves trimmed with natural sable cuffs. Mrs. Johnson wore a single strand of pearls with the dress.

PATRICIA RYAN NIXON wore a mimosa silk satin gown with a long-sleeved bolero jacket (third from right) at the inaugural ball of 1969 for President Richard M. Nixon.

Designed by Karen Stark of Harvey Berin, the dress features a bell-shaped skirt, sleeveless bodice, and a small stand-up collar and narrow cummerbund. Scrolls of gold and silver bullion are embroidered on the jacket, collar, and cummerbund, which are embellished with hand-set Austrian crystal jewels.

ELIZABETH (BETTY) BLOOMER FORD (fourth from right) added to the collection a dress she often wore at state affairs as First Lady. The dress was designed and made for her by Frankie Welch of Alexandria, Virginia. The fabric is a pale green chiffon embroidered with silk chrysanthemums highlighted with iridescent green sequins. The gown is made in princess lines with long sleeves and a stand-up collar and, as a concession to convenience, it fastens with a long zipper down the center front of the dress.

The blue dress which ROSALYNN SMITH CARTER (fifth from right) wore at President Jimmy Carter's presidential inaugural ball in January 1977 had first been worn in Georgia in 1971, six years before, at a ball given to celebrate Mr. Carter's inauguration as Governor of Georgia. The silk chiffon dress has a soft full skirt and full sleeves. It is trimmed at the waist and on the wristband with gold braid, and it has a narrow, stand-up collar covered with gold braid. Over the dress is a full-length sleeveless coat made of fabric woven with blue- and gold-colored threads.

NANCY DAVIS REAGAN (far left) wears her inaugural ball gown, a one-shouldered sheath designed by James Galanos. The white satin fabric of the dress is overlaid with lace having a fern motif with the leaves outlined in crystal and chalk beads and the stems of raised bugle beads. Beaded white satin pumps and long kid gloves complete the ensemble Mrs. Reagan wore to eight balls on January 20, 1981.

1961–1980s
Red Room

Jacqueline Kennedy

Lady Bird Johnson

Patricia Nixon

Betty Ford

Rosalynn Carter

Nancy Reagan

From left to right, shown here in reverse chronological order: Mrs. Reagan, Mrs. Carter, Mrs. Ford, Mrs. Nixon, Mrs. Johnson, and Mrs. Kennedy. (Red Room text, including descriptions of these First Ladies' dresses, is on the preceding page.)